DON'T WHIZ
ON AN
ELECTRIC
FENCE

GRANDPA'S
COUNTRY WISDOM

ROY ENGLISH

GIBBS SMITH
TO ENRICH AND...
Salt Lake City | Charles...

Revised Edition
13   20 19 18 17 16 15 14 13 12 11 10 9 8

Published by
Gibbs Smith
P.O. Box 667
Layton, Utah 84041

1.800.835.4993 orders
www.gibbs-smith.com

Design by Black Eye Design
Printed and bound in the U.S.A.
Gibbs Smith books are printed on either recycled, 100 percent
post-consumer waste, FSC-certified papers or on paper
produced from a 100 percent certified sustainable forest-
controlled wood source.

Library of Congress Cataloging-in-Publication Data

English, Roy, 1943-
   Don't whiz on an electric fence : grandpa's country wisdom /
Roy English. — 1st ed.
      p. cm.
   ISBN-13: 978-1-4236-0701-4
   ISBN-10: 1-4236-0701-5
   1. American wit and humor. I. Title.
   PN6162.E53 2009
   818'.5402—dc22

                                        2009017823

ISBN 13: 978-0-87905-755-8 (first edition)
ISBN 10: 0-87905-755-6 (first edition)

DON'T NAME A PIG YOU PLAN TO EAT.

EARLY TO BED
AND EARLY
TO RISE WILL
PRETTY MUCH
SHUT DOWN
THE DOMINO
GAME.

Trouble is
a private
thing;

don't lend
it, and don't
borrow it.

Country fences
need to be
horse high,
pig tight,
and bull strong.

THE WEATHER

can make a farmer look mighty
smart, or mighty dumb.

LIFE IS NOT ABOUT

how fast you run,
or how high you climb,

BUT HOW WELL YOU BOUNCE.

KEEP SKUNKS AND BANKERS AT A DISTANCE.

DON'T LET THE CHICKENS ROOST OVER THE WELL.

DON'T WEAR polyester to a wiener roast.

Life is simpler when you plow around the stumps.

NOTHIN' ON EARTH IS FINER THAN A GOOD, SLOW, TWO-INCH RAIN.

Mortgaging
a future
crop is
saddling a
wobbly colt.

A BUMBLE BEE IS FASTER THAN A JOHN DEERE TRACTOR.

DON'T STAND IN THE TROUGH WHEN YOU FEED THE PIGS.

Stuff tends
to break
when it's
loaned or
borrowed.

TROUBLE WITH
A MILK COW
IS THAT SHE
WON'T STAY
MILKED.

ALWAYS DANCE WITH THE
ONE WHO BRUNG YOU,

UNLESS IT IS YOUR COUSIN.

Don't gobble in the woods during hunting season.

Don't spread your blanket WHERE A CAT'S BEEN DIGGIN'.

DON'T SKINNY DIP WITH SNAPPIN' TURTLES.

The shallower
the stream,
the louder
the babble.

WORDS THAT SOAK INTO YOUR EARS ARE WHISPERED, NOT YELLED.

MEANNESS

don't

happen

overnight.

TO KNOW how country folks
are doing, look at their barns, not
their houses.

Never lay an angry hand
on a kid or an animal;
IT JUST AIN'T HELPFUL.

COUNTRY FOLKS will help a fella who is down on his luck, but they got no patience with freeloaders.

Hoot owls
and bankers
sleep with
ONE EYE
OPEN.

WHEN YOU'RE GREEN, YOU GROW. WHEN YOU THINK YOU ARE RIPE, YOU GET ROTTEN.

The only thing
worse than a
lawn mower
that won't start
is one that will.

FORGIVE YOUR ENEMIES.

★ ★ ★

IT MESSES WITH THEIR HEADS.

Goin' to bed
mad ain't
no fun, but
it's better
than fightin'
all night.

DON'T SELL YOUR MULE TO BUY A PLOW.

Two can live as cheap as one if one don't eat.

NO WOMAN IS TRULY FREE UNTIL SHE CAN CHANGE A FLAT TIRE.

FOLKS DON'T CHANGE. They just get more so.

DON'T CORNER SOMETHING THAT'S MEANER THAN YOU.

YOU CAN CATCH more flies with honey than vinegar, assuming you want to catch flies.

**MAN IS THE
ONLY CRITTER
WHO FEELS
THE NEED TO
LABEL THINGS
AS FLOWERS
OR WEEDS.**

It don't
take a very
big man
to carry a
grudge.

Don't go
hunting
with a fella
named
CHUG-A-LUG.

YOU CAN'T UNSAY A CRUEL THING.

IF IT AIN'T BROKE,
CHANCES ARE IT WILL BE.

Every path has
some puddles.

WHEN YOU WALLOW WITH PIGS, EXPECT TO GET DIRTY.

THE BEST SERMONS ARE LIVED, NOT PREACHED.

A fella who is
too quick with
an apology
likely screws
up a lot.

Most of
the stuff
folks worry
about
NEVER
HAPPENS.

LAZY AND QUARRELSOME
are ugly sisters.

THERE AIN'T a horsehair's
difference between begging and
borrowing.

Stumbling over the truth
can break a heart.

You can't blame a worm for
not wanting to go fishing.

A THREE-POUND CAT CAN EAT A FOUR-POUND FISH.

A FELLA will chase what runs, and run from what chases.

DON'T SNEEZE BEHIND A SKITTISH MULE.

Cow chips need
to dry out for
a spell before
you toss them.

A COUNTRY DOG NEVER FORGETS WHERE HE BURIED HIS BONE.

BEING NEIGHBORLY don't mean stickin' your nose in somebody's business.

NOTHING IS IMPOSSIBLE,

except peeing in a naked
man's pocket.

It's
downright
annoying to
argue with
a fella who
knows what
he's talking
about.

IF YOU RUN WITH HOUNDS, EXPECT TO GET FLEAS.

Coffee is
best when
it's saucered
and blowed.

A little tear
absorbs a
big pain.

YOU HAVE TO BUST SOME CLODS TO MAKE A CROP.

DON'T RIDE A NEW PATH AT FULL TROT.

An ignorant
fella is
hell-bent on
proving his
limitations.

SMALL
MINDS
AND BIG
MOUTHS
have a way
of hooking
up.

Debt is like
dragging a
rock in your
cotton sack.

IT'S HARD TO KEEP A BLANKET ON THE NAKED TRUTH.

COUNTRY FOLKS

laugh when you laugh,
cry when you cry,
know when you're sick,
and care when you die.

If at first you
don't succeed,
try raising
rabbits.

Don't fry frog legs in an open skillet.

DON'T SMOKE IN THE HAYLOFT.

FIREWOOD WARMS YOU TWICE:

WHEN YOU CUT IT AND
WHEN YOU BURN IT.

A mule can't
help it if his
daddy is a
JACKASS.

SOME FOLKS ARE LIKE DUCKS;

they seem to glide along easy because

you can't see how hard they work below

the surface.

COUNTRY FOLKS KNOW A LOT OF STUFF THAT AIN'T WROTE DOWN NOWHERE.

DON'T STAND BEHIND A COUGHING COW.

Better to
have loved
and lost
THAN TO
MARRY
A DAIRY
FARMER.

INTEREST ON DEBT NEVER SLEEPS.

THE DIFFERENCE BETWEEN
YOUNG LIARS AND OLD THIEVES

IS JUST A MATTER OF TIME.

Hunt every
varmint from
downwind,
except a
polecat.

IT'S HARD TO PLANT A SEEDLESS GRAPE.

THE SWEETEST PEACHES ARE JUST OUT OF REACH.

DON'T WHIZ ON AN ELECTRIC FENCE.

For rusty joints, try a little elbow grease.

AN OUNCE OF DOING IS WORTH A POUND OF TALK.

The acorn doesn't fall
far from the tree,
BUT SOME NUTS ROLL A LONG
WAY FROM THEIR ROOTS.

Don't rock back on a three-legged stool.

A YOUNG GIRL needs something to love when she is too old for dolls and too young for boys. A HORSE IS GOOD.

YOU CAN'T BURY A FELLA JUST BECAUSE HE HAS BEEN DEAD FOR YEARS.

A rooster does the crowing

WHILE THE HEN
DOES THE WORK.

COURTSHIP

is dancing

in the

moonlight;

MARRIAGE

is washing

socks.

SOME FOLKS HAVE TO SNORE IN SELF-DEFENSE.

WHEN A FELLA IS LATE FOR
WORK, he should do the right
thing and leave work early to
make up for it.

The world
could use a
good worry-
wart remover.

Some city
folks think
a square
meal is a
sandwich.

THE DIFFERENCE IN KNOW-HOW AND WISDOM IS IN THE DOING.

COUNTRY FOLKS CAN MAKE DO WITH MIGHTY LITTLE.

SOME FOLKS HAVE 20
YEARS OF EXPERIENCE;

others have one year of
experience 20 times.

IT'S EASIER
TO PATCH
A BROKEN
MIRROR THAN
A REPUTATION.

DIVORCE

changes

the tire;

MARRIAGE

fixes the

flat.

There are lots
of country
jobs, but few
positions.

FOLKS CAN SPOT A CITY FELLA A COUNTRY MILE AWAY.

Cream rises
to the top, but
so does some
other crud.

TURNIPS AND SWEET POTATOES will get you through a depression. Just ask Grandpa.

A CLINGING VINE CAN CHOKE A BODY.

Don't try to hold a barn cat against his will.

NO JACKASS

ever got ahead by kicking up his heels every night.

EVEN STUBBORN MULES KNOW YOU HAVE TO PULL TOGETHER.

THE BULL IS HALF THE SECRET
TO BUILDING A BETTER HERD.

SOME FELLAS HAVE MORE WISHBONE THAN BACKBONE.

THE ONLY THING WORSE

than finding a worm in your apple is

FINDING HALF A WORM.

DON'T SHARE A CROSSCUT SAW WITH A QUITTER.

When you feel
neighborly, dust
a little sugar
on your words
and cookies.

Little pigs make big hogs.

A WRINKLED BROW DON'T MEAN A WRINKLED HEART.

Riddle: What does it mean when a country preacher looks at his watch?

ANSWER: IT DON'T
MEAN NOTHIN'.

A FELLA CAN KILL HIMSELF WITH A FORK AND SPOON.

Whatever the illness, time is the best cure.

FEED A COLD, STARVE A FEVER, SOAK A THORN, AIR A WART.

Life is like juggling pitchforks:

everyone knows when you mess up.

IT'S BEST TO STOP TALKING

once you've said all you know.

If wishes
were horses,
some folks
would need
a lot of hay.

A FANCY TITLE IS ABOUT AS USEFUL AS THE CURL IN A PIG'S TAIL.

MOUNT A HORSE from the left,

milk a cow from the right,

approach a mule from the front,

a billy goat from the rear.

NOTHING SMELLS FRESHER
THAN CLEAN SHEETS
HUNG IN THE SUNSHINE.

A cat that licks
his paw may
be scratching
his tongue.

ADVICE MOST NEEDED IS LEAST HEEDED.

Grave marker in a country cemetery—

★ ★ ★

I TOLD Y'ALL I WAS SICK.

★ ★ ★

A FELLA can tell how happy he is going to be in twenty years by looking at his father-in-law.

You don't miss
the water till
you get an Alka
Seltzer hung in
your throat.

Some folks
would say
a lot more
if they
didn't talk
so much.

DON'T LICK A FROZEN PUMP HANDLE.